HOW TO GET RICH IF YOU'RE A BABY

HOW TO GET RICH IF YOU'RE A BABY

JOHN A. RUSSO

Burning Bulb
PUBLISHING

How to Get Rich if You're a Baby
by **John A. Russo**

Burning Bulb Publishing
P.O. Box 4721
Bridgeport, WV 26330-4721
www.BurningBulbPublishing.com

Paperback edition ISBN: 978-1-964172-58-3

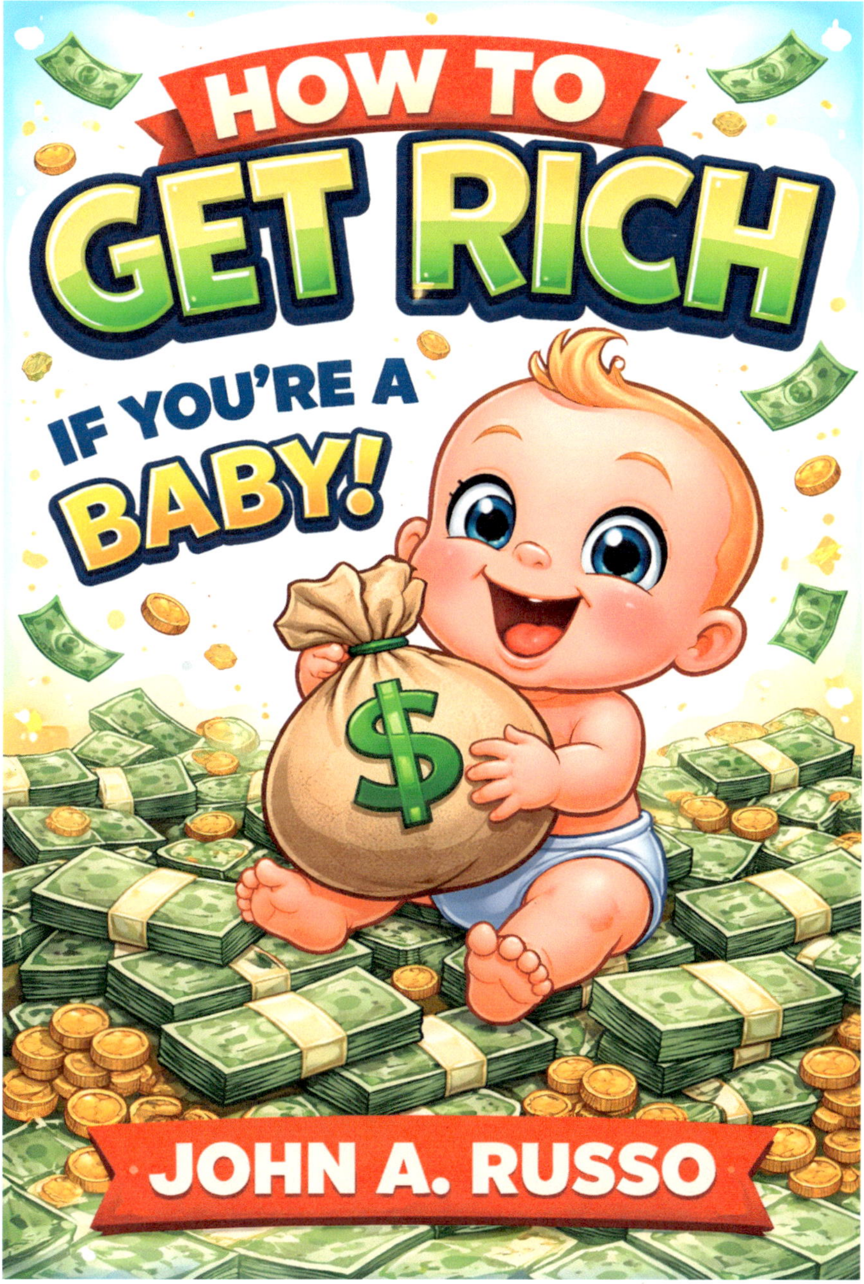
HOW TO
GET RICH
IF YOU'RE A
BABY!
$
JOHN A. RUSSO

NIGHT OF
LIVING DEAD

CHAPTER ONE

MY FINANCIAL PERILS AND MILESTONES

You might know me as the co-creator—along with George A. Romero and Russ Streiner—of the classic horror film *Night of the Living Dead.* Over a career that has now stretched more than sixty years, I've made sixteen feature films and published more than forty novels. And that's only a fraction of what I've written or created.

There were times when I made a good deal of money. There were also times when I was completely broke. What I never managed to achieve, however, was lasting financial security—at least not when it could have mattered most.

The entertainment business has a glamorous reputation, but behind that sheen lurks a darker reality. It attracts not only dreamers and artists, but also chiselers, con men, thieves, and opportunists of every stripe. I encountered them all. And like many creative people, I learned my most important financial lessons far too late.

If all I had ever wanted was financial comfort, I could have achieved it—even while pursuing my creative passions—by following principles I didn't understand until much later in life. It's too late for me to take full advantage of that knowledge now. But it is *not* too late for you. And it is certainly not too late for your child.

That is why this book exists.

I grew up in Clairton, Pennsylvania, a steel town about twelve miles from downtown Pittsburgh, though it felt a world away. My father worked as a millwright at U.S. Steel's Irvin Works, as did most of the men on our street. We lived in a modest company-built duplex—four rooms, a coal bin in the basement, and a bathroom that would make modern homeowners' shudder.

My parents used to tell me stories about their early struggles—how poor they once were, how they had stolen a potato from a landlady and split it between them, eating it raw. But by the time I came along, life felt stable. We weren't wealthy, but we had what everyone else around us had. During the postwar years, a single union job could support a family, send kids to college, and provide a sense of security that now feels almost mythical.

College was affordable then. My parents helped put me through West Virginia University, supplemented by a scholarship and summer jobs that paid less than a dollar an hour. I graduated in 1961 with a degree in English Education, fully expecting to become a teacher.

Then I met George Romero.

Through my closest friend, Rudy Ricci, I was introduced to George and Russ Streiner—young men just as obsessed with storytelling and movies as I was. George, in particular, believed with absolute certainty that movies could be made outside Hollywood. That idea was radical at the time.

After teaching fourth grade for less than a year and serving a two-year Army stint, I joined George and Russ at a small Pittsburgh production company called The Latent Image. The pay was terrible. The hours were brutal. We slept on studio floors between jobs. But we were learning everything—camera work, editing, sound, lighting, logistics—because we had to.

We were young, exhausted, and idealistic. And then one day, over lunch, everything changed.

The idea was absurdly simple. We had just purchased a used 35mm Arriflex camera. What if we pooled money from friends and family and made a feature film ourselves?

We were laughed at. Then people joined in.

We scraped together about $6,000 and made a horror movie that we believed could be better than the junk we were seeing on late-night television. Against all logic, *Night of the Living Dead* became a sensation. It opened in a handful of theaters and exploded from there, eventually becoming one of the highest-grossing independent horror films of all time.

It should have changed our lives financially.

It didn't.

Months went by without payment. When we finally received a profit-sharing check to the tune of $250,000—it seemed like a fortune. But it was split among thirty-three shareholders. Worse, it turned out to be almost the last meaningful payment we would ever receive.

We later discovered—through audits and litigation—that the distributor had made millions while paying us pennies. We sued and won. The company declared bankruptcy. We recovered the rights to our film, but not the money.

An executive from the distribution company once said, smirking, "We made millions from that movie, and paid them pennies."

That was my first major financial lesson: success does not equal security. Ownership matters. Knowledge matters. And trust—especially in business—must be earned, not assumed.

In the movie business, you don't usually have a regular paycheck, especially if you are a freelancer. Money comes to you in dribs and drabs and sometimes in larger amounts that are like windfalls.

When I participated in a film-convention panel with Bruce Campbell, the actor who launched his career by starring in *The Evil Dead*, he said, "When you land a major role, you get really big checks – but then you have to live off of them for the next two or three years."

That is why some people who suddenly get that big Hollywood money quickly go broke. They think that they've made it now, and the money will keep coming. Then it doesn't.

In my own case, I didn't throw money away. I paid off bills, including car payments and credit card debt. Lacking a financial education, I didn't think about investing. I didn't throw it away, but I failed to invest it. Each time I paid off most of my monthly bills, I hoped stability would somehow take care of itself. It never does.

Looking back now, I can see a pattern stretching across my entire career. I took enormous creative risks. I worked harder than most people I knew. I experienced success that many would envy.

But I never learned early what I should have learned first: how money grows, how money is protected, and how devastating ignorance can be.

That realization—painful and humbling—sets the stage for everything that follows in these pages.

Because the most important financial lesson I ever learned came far too late. And it doesn't have to for you—or for your child.

CHAPTER TWO

WE CONTINUE TO STRUGGLE

On the surface, things began to look better after *Night of the Living Dead,* in spite of the ripoff by our distributor. For about ten months, our small, energetic group was on what might be called a "sugar high."

The notoriety from the film brought work. The Latent Image started landing larger commercial jobs—television spots, industrial films, and promotional projects that paid far better than the shoestring work we had done before. For the first time, George Romero, Russ Streiner, Vince Survinski, Gary Streiner, and I were earning what could reasonably be called "decent salaries."

We used a portion of that long-awaited distributor check to pay off debts incurred during the making of *Night.* Some bonuses were handed out. Spirits lifted. It felt, finally, like the struggle phase was behind us.

I got engaged to Mary Lou Andrews, the woman who would soon become my wife, now that I could comfortably afford to give her the kind of wedding that would satisfy our large extended families. The wedding was set for July of 1969. For the first time since entering the movie business, I felt cautiously optimistic.

That optimism would not last.

Even as *Night of the Living Dead* continued to play across the country—and as we later learned, continued to generate profits for everyone except us—we were already looking ahead. We wanted to prove that we were more than horror filmmakers. We believed we could make any kind of movie.

At the time, youthful, counterculture films such as *The Graduate*, *Easy Rider*, *Goodbye, Columbus*, and *Alice's Restaurant* were dominating the box office. We believed we were just as capable of capturing that spirit.

I proposed a plan: The Latent Image would contribute approximately $100,000 in goods and services, and we would raise another $100,000 in cash from investors. I prepared a full investment proposal for a film written by Rudy Ricci titled *At Play with the Angels*, complete with photos, press clippings, and detailed projections.

Thanks largely to the notoriety of *Night of the Living Dead*, we succeeded in raising the money. Production began in the summer of 1969, literally the day after my bachelor party.

Unfortunately, from the start, the project was plagued by ego clashes, creative disagreements, and internal tensions that had been quietly building for some time. What should have been a proving ground for our collective talent became instead a slow-motion unraveling.

The breakup was not sudden—it was a gradual erosion of trust, shared purpose, and unity. Russ Streiner, Gary Streiner, and I eventually left the company. Vince Survinski and George Romero remained.

I don't recount this with bitterness. It was another hard lesson in the realities of collaboration. Success doesn't always bond people—it can fracture them. When there is money, prestige, or recognition at stake, even the strongest alliances can falter.

As my attorney later put it, "When somebody breaks out of the pack, they don't want it to be you. They want it to be themselves."

Financially, I found myself back where I had started—scrambling.

Mary Lou and I were newly married. She worked as a technical illustrator, earning about $7,000 a year. I earned money sporadically, piecing together income from freelance writing, editing, and short-term film work. There was no safety net. There was no long-term plan.

Luckily, good friends came to my rescue.

Don Redinger, an experienced independent filmmaker and a generous mentor, hired me to write scripts for a series of worldwide travel films produced under his company, Travel Lore. Russ Streiner, after forming Streiner Films LLC, hired me for crew and post-production work on his projects.

These jobs kept me afloat, but they didn't provide stability.

Still, the dream refused to die.

In 1971, I completed a screenplay titled *Bonner*, inspired by the mass shooting at the University of Texas. Around the same time, Rudy Ricci finished a screenplay and novel titled *Johnny Hurrah*, centered on a Vietnam veteran's struggle to reintegrate into civilian life.

We decided to package both projects together and seek financing. Our plan was straightforward: raise approximately $1.5 million per picture, make the films, and then go our separate ways. We asked Russ Streiner to join us because his producer credit on *Night of the Living Dead* strengthened our credibility.

That decision led us directly into another financial disaster.

Through a high school connection, we were introduced to Lynn P. Dunn, president of a financing firm called LPD Equity, and his associate Herb Wagner. They lavished praise on our credentials and offered to raise $3 million—on one condition.

We would need to form a permanent corporation so they could sell stock.

Reluctantly, we agreed.

To "get the ball rolling," Dunn and Wagner suggested we put up some seed money. I borrowed $15,000 from a close friend, depositing it into the account of our newly formed company, New American Films, Inc.

Within days, the money was gone.

Dunn and Wagner had drained the account.

When confronted, they dismissed the theft as "chicken feed." When I demanded the money be returned, they refused.

Then things became surreal.

One night, a bomb exploded in Lynn Dunn's Cadillac while it was parked outside a Pittsburgh supper club. The bomb-maker blew off his own arm. Dunn survived, shaken but unharmed.

The FBI descended—and because of our recent financial dispute, *we* became suspects.

Suddenly, instead of pitching films, we were defending ourselves against accusations of attempted murder. Investors vanished overnight. New American Films, which had barely been born, now had two feet in its grave.

Eventually, the real perpetrators were caught. Their motive had nothing to do with us—they were trying to collect on a $250,000 insurance policy on Dunn's life.

But the damage on me, Rudy and Russ was irreversible.

Despite clearing our names of the bombing and attempted murder when the true culprits were put in prison, New American Films never recovered from people's suspicions. Trust in us by the business community was largely gone. Momentum was halted. Opportunities evaporated.

Still, we didn't immediately give up. We tried to keep the company alive—partly out of stubbornness, partly out of hope.

Looking back, it was another mistake.

What I failed to understand then—and what I understand all too well now—is that perseverance alone is not enough. There are moments when cutting losses is the smartest financial decision a person can make.

I didn't know that yet.

What I *was* learning—slowly and painfully—was that creative success does not protect you from financial ruin. Passion does not substitute for knowledge. And trust, once broken, can destroy not only partnerships but futures.

I was still chasing opportunity. I was still creating. And I was still financially vulnerable.

The next chapter would show me just how dangerous that combination could be.

Yum!
Baby Food!

CHAPTER THREE

MY NEXT LOW-BUDGET MOVIE

By the early 1970s, desperation had become a familiar companion.

New American Films was wounded but not yet officially dead. We had equipment, a small office, and just enough momentum left to convince ourselves that one good idea could turn everything around. What we lacked was capital—and time.

It was during this period that I came up with what was either a stroke of comic genius or a symptom of financial panic.

One day I walked into Russ Streiner's office and said, "If companies are making dildos, vibrators, and all manner of exotic sex products, then somebody has to be testing them. So why not make a movie about those testers—and how screwed up their lives are, even though they can't figure out why?"

Rudy Ricci, who was sitting across from Russ, burst out laughing and literally fell out of his chair. The idea hit a nerve. Sex comedies were popular, satire was fashionable, and—most importantly—we could make the movie cheaply.

We titled it *The Liberation of Cherry Jankowski.*

Using New American's office as the fictional "Joyful Products, Inc.," we transformed our limited resources into production assets. Rudy played Marcello Fettucini, the former "Number One Male Product Tester," whose career was collapsing because he could no longer perform. Russ and I portrayed a pair of lecherous, half-deranged scientists. Around them revolved a cast of bizarre characters: a peeping Tom, a dirty-phone caller with a stutter, a perverted psychiatrist, and other grotesque caricatures of a supposedly liberated society.

By this point, we had already invested in basic production equipment using some of the money raised from New American's stock offering. That allowed us to shoot and edit the film in 16mm for roughly $20,000. We later scraped together another $15,000 for a 35mm blowup.

A Pittsburgh theater catering to college audiences booked the film for a two-week run, paying us $10,000. The movie got solid laughs. It didn't offend people so much as amuse them. For the first time in a while, we had a tangible win.

It wasn't much—but it was something.

Months later, that "something" opened a door.

I landed a meeting with Sam Sherman, president of Independent-International Pictures. Sam was riding high at the time, having turned a modest sex comedy called *Soap* into a major hit by retitling it *The Boob Tube* and marketing it brilliantly.

Sam loved our movie.

"It's worthy of Woody Allen," he told me.

Then he said something that would define the next phase of my career: "Let's repackage it."

He proposed a new title—*The Booby Hatch*—and asked me to write and direct about ten minutes of new material to heighten the sex and comedy. When I told him we had no money left, he didn't flinch.

"I'll give you four thousand dollars for the new scenes," he said. "And another thousand for you personally —so you don't have to work under duress."

Then he called down the hall and told his partner to cut me a check.

That moment mattered far more than the amount.

Sam Sherman was one of the rare honest men in the movie business. He understood marketing, understood how to invent catchy, money-making titles, and understood how perception could transform a film's fate. He despised charlatans and prided himself on telling the same story, the *true* story, to everyone he met, so he wouldn't have to remember an assortment of lies. He said, "Talent is almost never enough if you don't understand presentation and timing." We became close friends and remained so until his death decades later.

Under Sam's guidance, *The Booby Hatch* found modest success. It wasn't enough to finance another feature, but it kept us viable. It proved we could still make movies, still attract distributors, still survive.

However, despite its relative success, the film eventually ran into a familiar problem. It was too tame for adult theaters and too erotic for "family" theaters. Many major newspapers refused to run our ads. Although it did well everywhere it was booked, we ran out of places that would book it. Meantime, the distribution landscape was changing rapidly, with major studios squeezing independent distributors out of the market.

Still, over time, the film turned a small profit.

And sometimes, success has side effects.

We cast David Emge in *The Booby Hatch* as a small-time gangster. George Romero noticed his performance and later cast him in *Dawn of the Dead.* That is the strange alchemy of the creative world—one small role can lead to a life-changing opportunity.

What mattered most to me, though, was that we stayed in the game.

I often think of a Theodore Roosevelt quote: "The man in the arena is the one who deserves the prize – he whose face is marred by dust and sweat and blood, who dares greatly even if he fails." That idea resonated with me then, and it still does. Courage alone does not build financial security – but I was in the arena, battling the winds of fortune.

My parents had never run a business. They had saved through checking accounts and CDs, cautiously avoiding risk. When I left teaching to make movies, they were terrified. They were proud of *Night of the Living Dead*, but they didn't understand the life I had chosen—and in truth, neither did I, at least financially.

Even when money came in, I didn't know how to make it grow.

Looking back, I can see how unprepared I was. I had talent. I had work ethic. I had resilience. What I lacked was a financial education.

I did not understand investing. I did not understand compounding. I did not understand how early decisions echo across decades.

Those realizations would come later—after more struggle, more near-successes, and one painful lesson that finally forged clarity.

That lesson is where the next chapter begins.

CHAPTER FOUR

MY THIRD SHOT AT THE BRASS RING

By the mid-1970s, perseverance had become both my strength and my liability.

New American Films was finally finished. After five years of effort, during which I rarely earned more than $5,000 annually, the company folded. One by one, the people involved drifted away—some to better-paying jobs, others to more stable careers. Eventually, I was alone with the wreckage of another failed venture.

I formed a new company, Market Square Productions, Inc., this time as the sole owner. I had learned enough to know that permanent partnerships carried too many risks I no longer wanted to shoulder. I agreed to collaborate with Paul McCollough on a project-by-project basis, splitting profits without binding ourselves to an equal partnership.

From 1976 to 1980, we managed to survive by producing television commercials and sales films. It wasn't glamorous, but it paid the bills. During that period, I wrote a screenplay initially called *The Vampire Cage,* about a family of satanists and their innocent victims. I thought it was pretty good, but I didn't know exactly how I was going to market it.

Then opportunity knocked again—unexpectedly.

Don Redinger, the same friend who had helped me survive earlier lean years, called to say his company, Travelore, had $35,000 sitting idle. He didn't want to lose a large portion of it to taxes and asked if I had a script worth investing in.

I said, "Yeah. Coincidentally, I just wrote one that can be filmed on the cheap, but it's tailor-made for me to make it look like it had a bigger budget."

When I pitched him on the creepy plot of *The Vampire Cage*, Don agreed to put up the money. I then contacted Sam Sherman at Independent-International Pictures, and Sam offered to match Don's investment—but with a crucial condition: the movie had to be shot in 35mm. That decision instantly raised the stakes. Twice as costly as 16mm.

Not only would I have to shoot it in 35mm for only $70,000 but Sam said the picture would also need a name actor in the cast, and he recommended Lawrence Tierney, whose fee and expenses consumed a meaningful chunk of the budget – over $4,000. Post-production would require a New York sound mix for about $6,000. I was undertaking a monumental task.

We shot the film under all that pressure, stretching our resources to the breaking point. The advantage, I believed, was that we already had distribution. Independent-International would release the film. No more hoping and no more praying to find a distributor after making ourselves "sick" to the tune of $70,000. Or so I thought.

But the rug got pulled out from under me. After coming up with a great campaign and changing the title of the movie to *Midnight,* Sam held onto the movie for nearly two years before releasing it. He insisted timing was everything. Slasher films were flooding the market, and he didn't want *Midnight* to bed lost in the glut and the clamor.

I hated waiting, but Sam was right. When *Midnight* finally opened in 1982, it earned a modest but respectable profit. Over time, it began to be hailed as a "cult classic."

In retrospect, *Midnight* represents both a victory and a warning. It proved I could still make feature films under brutal constraints. But it also reinforced a painful truth: even success, when under-capitalized, does not translate into security.

However, around this same time, my long involvement with *Return of the Living Dead* seemed poised to finally pay off.

Through attorneys and connections—including Frank Sinatra's inner circle—a deal was arranged for Sinatra to invest three million dollars into the film, with me directing. I was flown to Las Vegas and put up at Caesar's Palace. For the first time, it felt like the brass ring was truly within reach.

Then tragedy struck. Sinatra's mother was killed in a plane crash. The deal collapsed overnight.

This huge disappointment caused Tom Fox to ask if he could buy out my share, along with those of Russ Streiner and Rudy Ricci, for $250,000. My portion was approximately $83,000—the largest sum I had ever earned in the movie business.

This should have been a turning point.

It wasn't.

I did not squander the money. I paid off debts. I reduced credit card balances. And I managed to hang onto a $15,000 remainder which I intended to invest in an IRA, or preferably a Keough by relying on advice from bank officials who turned out to be mistaken about tax-avoidance deadlines. And because of their bad advice, I lost over $10,000 to taxes I should not have had to pay. Which devastated my savings account.

Still, I continued working. I had no choice, had to bite the bullet and keep working.

In 1985, I wrote and produced *The Majorettes*, which was sold for big bucks all over the world. I negotiated contracts carefully, insisting on a percentage of gross rather than net profits. I had learned that lesson well. But even then, promised returns failed to materialize. To date, I have never received any statements or checks.

Once again, success passed through my hands without staying.

Then, finally, real money arrived.

In 1989, I earned approximately $100,000, mostly due to writing and directing *Heartstopper,* which George Romero called "the most unique vampire movie since Salem's Lot." In 1990, largely due to the *Night of the Living Dead* remake, I earned about $300,000. My earnings in those two years gave me the chance to build a genuine nest egg.

This time, I knew enough to be cautious.

After paying taxes and necessary expenses, I invested a substantial portion of what remained into an annuity that guaranteed an annual return of 8.2 percent. It wasn't flashy, but it was stable. And it worked.

Over the next decade, that investment grew significantly. Combined with other holdings, my nest egg approached half a million dollars.

For the first time, I felt secure.

And then—disaster.

While I was deeply immersed in production of a gangster film, *The Mob Boss and the Soul Singer,* my financial advisor contacted me with what he described as a "terrific opportunity." He told me I should transfer my money into "a better-paying annuity" with a bonus of $5,000 and a guaranteed return—slightly lower, but still "safe."

I warned him: "That money is my safety net. I don't want to risk it."

He assured me it was protected.

It wasn't.

After the events of September 11th, the market collapsed. When my next statement arrived, nearly two-thirds of my money was gone. The guarantees applied only to the annuity value, not the cash value. The distinction had never been explained.

I had been "churned."

The advisor had earned a fat commission. I had lost my future.

That moment changed everything.

For the first time, I fully grasped how devastating ignorance about money could be. Not bad luck. Not lack of talent. Not lack of effort.

Ignorance.

Only then did I truly begin to understand compound interest, the Rule of 72, and the brutal advantage of time. Only then did I see how early knowledge could have changed everything.

That realization—painful and permanent—is what leads directly into the central idea of this book.

Because if I had understood these principles when I was young…

If someone had acted on them when I was a baby…

My financial story—and perhaps my life—would have been very different.

Everything I've described up to this point—every success, every betrayal, every missed opportunity—leads directly to one unavoidable conclusion: I did not lose financial security because I lacked talent, persistence, or opportunity. I lost it because I did not understand, early enough, how money grows. Only much later did I come to grasp a principle so simple, so powerful, and so overlooked that it could have changed everything for me if it had been applied when I was young—or better yet, when I was a baby. What follows is the core idea that finally brought all those hard-earned lessons into focus.

YEARS
8
16
24
32
40
48

CHAPTER FIVE

THE REAL AND FOREVER 15% TAX BREAK

What if there were a simpler way to provide long-term financial security than the systems we rely on today? What if, instead of depending entirely on government programs, individuals could build a foundation that could last a lifetime, without constant worry about whether it would be enough?

Such an approach would also have wider effects. Employers would keep more of what they pay in payroll taxes, and self-employed individuals would retain a larger share of their income.

This kind of "miracle" cannot happen overnight. But it *can* happen.

The system I have in mind takes advantage of the most powerful and reliable method of building wealth ever devised: **compound interest**. We all know, at least intellectually, that the money we invest earliest grows the most by the time we retire. Yet our current Social Security system completely ignores this fact.

Contributions are based on annual income. Since most people earn the most money later in life, they end up contributing the largest amounts precisely when those dollars have the least amount of time to grow. The result is that the power of time is largely lost.

It would be far better to contribute fewer dollars—but to do it early. As early as possible. Ideally, from the very beginning of life.

THE BABY ADVANTAGE

What if every child born in America had $1,000 invested on their behalf the day they entered the world?

Stay with me for a moment while I show you how that money could grow over a lifetime—and then I'll explain where that initial investment could come from.

The **Rule of 72** provides an easy way to estimate how long it takes an investment to double. Simply divide 72 by the annual rate of return, and the result tells you approximately how many years it will take for your money to double.

For example, if a newborn baby has $1,000 invested at 9 percent interest, that investment would double roughly every eight years:

Investment	Age
$1,000	Birth
$2,000	8
$4,000	16
$8,000	24
$16,000	32
$32,000	40
$64,000	48
$128,000	56

Investment	Age
$256,000	64
$512,000	72

With a "measly" $1,000 investment at birth, every American could retire at age seventy-two with more than half a million dollars—*without adding another penny*. If the return averaged 10 percent instead of 9 percent, that same person could reach that level in their early sixties.

That is the awesome power of time.

WHERE WOULD THE MONEY COME FROM?

The initial $1,000 could come from the parents. In exchange, they would forgo the current child tax deduction—approximately $600 per year—for as many years as necessary to reimburse the government for the investment.

The initial amount could also be modestly adjusted over time to account for inflation, ensuring that future generations receive an equivalent advantage.

The benefits of such a system would be enormous.

THE ADVANTAGES

1. **It would eliminate much of the Social Security bureaucracy.**

   The funds could be invested through regulated brokerages, insurance companies, or annuities—whatever vehicles make the most sense at the time.

2. **It would create massive tax savings.**

Corporations and individuals would no longer need to pay Social Security taxes at current levels.

3. **It would turn every American into a saver and investor.**

   Instead of relying on a pay-as-you-go system, capital would be accumulating and working for each individual, strengthening the entire economy.

4. **It would provide real social security.**

   People would own their retirement funds outright, freeing them from constant anxiety about whether benefits will be cut or eliminated.

5. **It would change the psychology of aging.**

   Instead of fearing later years, people could view them as opportunities to continue compounding wealth. Working an extra seven or eight years could double a nest egg.

As an added benefit, these funds could also help address health care and long-term care costs later in life, reducing the burden on taxpayers when individuals face medical or nursing-home expenses without sufficient resources.

WHY THIS MATTERS

The details of tax codes, interest rates, and government programs will always change. But the principle never does.

Money invested early grows more than money invested later.

Time is the greatest ally wealth can have.

And ignoring that truth is one of the most expensive mistakes a society—or an individual—can make.

CHAPTER SIX

REFLECTIONS UPON MY ESSAY

It has been about fifteen years since I first wrote *The Real and Forever 15% Tax Break*. Some of what were facts at the time I wrote that essay may no longer be as relevant today. But the **Rule of 72** still works.

Our Social Security system still operates on the assumption that millions of young workers will continue entering the workforce and paying into the system at levels sufficient to support retired citizens. As I write this, however, entry-level job markets are depressed, inflation has surged, and it has become increasingly difficult for young people to achieve what used to be called the American Dream.

Many young people no longer expect to do better than their parents did.

That reality raises an uncomfortable question: Will there be enough well-paid workers in the future to sustain our current Social Security system?

I am not an economist. I am not a financier. I am not a stock-market wizard. When I first published the essay you have just read, I hoped that knowledgeable people would critique it—poke holes in it, suggest improvements, or even tear it apart entirely. I believed that, at the very least, it might spark discussion and debate.

That didn't happen.

Still, I continue to believe the essay made valid and important points. Its true value lies not in whether every detail of the proposal could be implemented exactly as written, but in its central purpose: to wake people up to the necessity of saving and investing **as early as possible**.

Some years after publishing the essay, I came across newspaper articles written by people who were thinking along similar lines.

In 1994, *Newsweek* published an article by Joe Klein titled *If Chile Can Do It, Why Can't America Privatize Its Social Security System?* Klein told the story of Eduardo Silva, a Chilean citizen who was asked to give up his state-funded pension and instead contribute to a new system in which his retirement savings would be invested in regulated private funds.

Silva was initially skeptical, but he agreed to participate. Over thirteen years, his investment grew at an average annual rate of 14 percent. By age sixty-five, he was on track to retire with a pension larger than his working salary.

Klein described Chile's system as one of the first major social-policy innovations to emerge from the Southern Hemisphere, noting that it deserved serious consideration as the American system "slid toward financial and demographic catastrophe."

The following year, in 1995, the *Pittsburgh Post-Gazette* published an article by Sam Beard titled *REAL Social Security*. Beard began by acknowledging a growing national anxiety:

"Many of us are afraid that our future opportunity is diminishing. We are worried about our jobs and our standard of living. We are afraid that we are harming our children's chances."

Beard pointed out that when the baby boom generation began retiring, the existing pay-as-you-go Social Security system would be strained to the breaking point unless taxes were raised or benefits cut.

He proposed a system that would retain Social Security as a mandatory savings program but convert it from a pay-as-you-go model into a funded system—one in which individuals would own their own retirement accounts and choose private investment managers.

"This money would be in your name," Beard wrote. "You would own it."

Participants could also choose to purchase annuities with their accumulated capital, providing higher lifetime retirement income. By harnessing compound interest, Beard argued, the new system could ease the pressure on Social Security by allowing investment income—not just tax revenue—to fund benefits.

He estimated that by 2025, more than $100 billion per year in benefits could be paid from accumulated capital rather than government transfers.

Beard also addressed a source of public frustration that remains relevant today:

"It makes us angry when the government takes billions out of the Social Security trust fund to pay other debts. People instinctively know that this is wrong—because they would go to jail for doing the same thing."

His conclusion mirrored my own thinking. While Social Security surpluses exist, he argued, they should be used to help fund individual accounts rather than disappear into general government spending.

Reading these articles reassured me that my thinking was not radical or isolated. Others, many far more credentialed than I, were arriving at similar conclusions through their own analysis.

Whether or not large-scale reform ever occurs, the lesson remains unchanged.

Compound interest works.

Time magnifies its power.

And money invested early has an overwhelming advantage over money invested late. That truth applies to governments, corporations, families, and individuals alike.

FUTURE

CHAPTER SEVEN

BASIC POINTS TO PONDER

I often recall a piece of financial advice given to me by one of my favorite people, James Martell. Jim had been my high-school physics instructor and later became the principal of the school where I taught a fourth-grade class after leaving the Army.

Jim was bright, caring, and charismatic. In his gruffly warm, avuncular manner, he once said to me, "John, take a twenty-dollar bill out of your pay each month and put it into a savings account. Believe me, it adds up. I wish I had done it when I was your age."

At the time, I was taking home a little over three hundred dollars a month. That money barely lasted two weeks. By the end of the month, I was broke—mostly from chasing girls and having a good time, like most young men do. My brother and I shared a cheap apartment in Clairton, and he was earning three times what I was making at the Irvin Works of U.S. Steel.

How, I wondered, was I supposed to put aside twenty dollars a month without living like a monk in sackcloth and ashes?

Just for laughs, I'll share another piece of advice Jim Martell gave me when I was twenty-four.

"Marry a schoolteacher, John," he said. "They marry just as good as anybody else, and you'll have that extra income coming in."

Years later, teachers' unions fought hard battles to secure better wages and benefits, and today teachers are paid far better than they were when I first entered the workforce. When I started at The Latent Image, I was making exactly the same salary I had earned as a teacher—$325 per month.

Looking back, I realize that if I *had* listened to Jim and set aside even twenty dollars a month, it would have added up to a meaningful sum over time. An advertisement from my bank, PNC Bank in Pittsburgh, later drove that point home.

THE POWER OF SMALL AMOUNTS

At an average annual rate of 2 percent, compounded once per year:

- Save **$10 each week for 10 years**, and you'll have **$5,808**
- Save an **additional $25 each week for 10 years**, and you'll have **$14,519**
- Save an **additional $50 each week for 10 years**, and you'll have **$29,039**

These numbers may not sound life-changing, but they represent something far more important than the dollar amounts themselves: proof that consistency matters.

In 2010, Ryan Guina published an article in *Yahoo Finance* titled *A Simple Way to Become Wealthy*. Ryan began investing at nineteen while serving in the United States Air Force, but only after being prodded by a senior member of his squadron.

Like many young people, Ryan didn't believe he earned enough to invest. His mentor corrected him.

"Saving and investing isn't hard," the mentor said. "You just have to treat it like a bill. When your paycheck comes in, you pay your bills, right? Do the same thing with investing."

The advice was simple: divide the maximum IRA contribution by twelve and invest that amount each month. Better yet, automate it so you never have to think about it.

Ryan followed the advice—and it worked.

"It turns out he was right," Ryan wrote. "It wasn't that I didn't have enough money to invest. I just wasn't prioritizing how I used my money."

Ryan identified three reasons why automatic investing works so well:

1. **It's easy.** You don't have to remember to do it.
2. **It reinforces long-term discipline.** You remove emotion and hesitation from the process.
3. **It eliminates the need to outsmart the market.** Most people fail when they try.

Those points align perfectly with everything I learned the hard way.

The lesson here is not about becoming rich overnight. It's about habits—small, boring, repeatable habits that quietly shape a future.

Most people don't fail financially because they make one catastrophic mistake. They fail because they never establish a system that works on their behalf month after month, year after year.

That realization leads directly to the next and final chapter, where the focus turns to children—and how early education about money can change lives.

CHAPTER EIGHT

RAISING MONEY-WISE TODDLERS

In recent years, there has been a growing interest in teaching children about money, and I'm encouraged by that trend.

When I was a student at West Virginia University, one of my favorite courses was an eight-credit class called Social Science. I've long believed that the subjects covered in that course should be taught not just to college students, but to children—first in simple terms, and then in increasingly complex ways as they grow.

The course was divided into eight-week segments, each taught by one of the university's top experts. One segment focused on Soviet Russia's system of government, presented objectively rather than ideologically. Another examined American democracy. Yet another explored the criminal justice system.

At first, many of us students laughed when we were told that one segment would be devoted to *Marriage and the Family*. Who needed to learn about that?

It turned out to be one of the most valuable and eye-opening parts of the entire course. It became painfully clear that money problems were a leading cause of failed marriages—often ending in divorce or worse. That realization stayed with me and reinforced my belief that financial education should begin far earlier in life.

Apparently, I'm not alone in that belief.

Warren Buffett—one of the wealthiest, wisest, and most socially conscious investors in the world—recognized the same need. In an interview with *Yahoo Finance*, he discussed his involvement in an animated series for children called *Secret Millionaires Club*, which also featured voices such as Jay-Z and Shaquille O'Neal.

Buffett explained that the goal of the series had nothing to do with amassing wealth for its own sake. Instead, it was about helping children develop healthy financial habits that would serve them throughout their lives.

"The best investment you can make is an investment in yourself," Buffett said. "The more you learn, the more you earn."

Through relatable stories and adventures, the series teaches kids how money works, how businesses function, and how thoughtful decision-making can lead to positive outcomes. It also engages parents and teachers, making financial education a shared experience.

Neale Godfrey, one of the first female executives at Chase Manhattan Bank and a *New York Times* best-selling author of *Money Doesn't Grow on Trees*, has spent decades advocating for early financial education. She later founded the Children's Financial Network, Inc., to further that mission.

In a 2018 interview published in *The Nuveen Investor*, Godfrey emphasized that most children learn only one thing about money: how to spend it.

"They need to learn how to earn it, how to save it, how to give to charity, and how to spend it wisely," she said.

Godfrey also pointed out that many families underestimate the future costs their children will face. A four-year private college education can easily approach $400,000.

"When kids start saying 'I want, I want,' which happens around age three," she explained, "that's when money lessons should begin. Children need to understand that money is earned. There is no entitlement program that magically provides everything."

She also cautioned parents not to confuse net worth with self-worth. Money is a tool, not a measure of human value.

Godfrey stressed the importance of using everyday experiences as teaching moments.

When you use a credit card instead of cash, explain what a credit card actually is—and the costs associated with it. When you write a check or pay a bill online, explain what those transactions mean. Children should understand that money is not a magic substance that appears without consequences.

"If you make your world a classroom," Godfrey said, "children will naturally connect money and investing to the products and services around them."

My own bank, PNC Bank, has taken similar steps by producing educational materials such as *Teach Your Kids to Be Financially Responsible* and *Simple Ways to Teach Children About Money.*

One recommendation is to introduce young children to actual coins and bills so they can understand their value. Once they grasp that concept, they can be encouraged to save coins in a piggy bank.

PNC also suggests taking children on a "money tour" of your home. Many children have no idea how much furniture costs, or that turning up the heat increases energy bills.

Another important concept is saving. Parents are encouraged to require children to save a portion—perhaps 25 to 50 percent—of any money they receive. Opening a savings account in a child's name and explaining compound interest can make an abstract idea tangible.

PNC offers several general guidelines for parents:

- **Set a good example.** Children absorb financial habits by watching their parents.

- **Teach one lesson at a time.** Avoid overwhelming children with too much information at once.
- **Look for everyday learning opportunities.** Shopping trips, ATM visits, and bill payments can all become teaching moments.

Financial education doesn't have to be complicated. It simply has to begin.

CLOSING THOUGHTS

It is my sincere hope that I've shown you some ways to avoid the worst mistakes I've made, while also giving you ideas for building a more secure future for yourself and your family.

As you teach your children about money, don't forget to show them that life is meant to be enjoyed. In spite of the rough spots in my long career, I never lost my enthusiasm. Even now, I still wake up fired up with ideas—just as I did when I was five years old.

Every day is a gift.

That feeling was captured perfectly in a passage from one of Rex Stout's *Nero Wolfe* novels. In a moment of despair, an old friend blurts out, "Life! I'm afraid I don't know what life is!"

And Wolfe replies, "Sir! You do know! It is the amenities."

May you always enjoy the amenities—while building a future secure enough to protect them.

Made in the USA
Monee, IL
05 November 2026

67385756R00029